"*Bedding Vows* are love poems. Make no mistake about it – love of earth and mate and how they cast their lots – wrapped into sensual images of daily living, all the while inviting ours with straight talk. Ranzoni writes with perfection, packs in content with ease, and models how delicious life can be. She delivers a grateful feast."

   - **H.H. Price and George N. Price** - she, a native New England writer, co-author of *Maine's Visible Black History*; and he, a long term pastor in Ranzoni's county – they, mates of 50 years.

"Discovering in my own backyard a poet really living, eating, breathing poetry was a refreshing surprise! More delightful still is this collection of love poems. Sometimes for the land she works and inhabits, sometimes for the divorced but never departed, and sometimes for her husband and lover, every line is honest and purely insightful. The reader is led to believe all this passion for people and place are her own, not the poet's. In the end, they indeed become so."

   - **Kimberly Pye**, native outback Bucksport Mainer and young wife working in China. Teacher, freelance writer, blogger, author of *Poems from the sky, literally,* and *Rambling: Poems for Here, There, and Home.*

"Since I was like 'the boy riding his bike by to tread his uncle's hay,' I can corroborate the down home truth in Patricia Ranzoni's earthy, amusing, and powerful poetry in *Bedding Vows*. Pat always writes movingly about the two great human needs of love and work and how they go together. Whether about the making of buck neck stew, buying a mermaid for the bird bath, eating haddock sandwiches, or celebrating a couple still madly in love after years of marriage, Ranzoni's great love for her husband, family, farm, and Downeast heritage are well on display in this wonderfully readable and re-readable collection."

   - **Sanford Phippen**, lifelong Mainer, University of Maine English instructor, writers of Maine historian, author of *The Police Know Everything, People Trying to be Good,* and *Kitchen Boy.*

"Ranzoni's well-chosen title provides a lens through which a reader's understanding is focused. *Bedding Vows* alerts us to her proposition that lasting love is embedded not only in the intimate details of a particular shared life but also in the couple's generational and cultural connections, providing context for that enduring relationship. Through sensitive and evocative images, Ranzoni creates a poignant picture of a maturing love that, based on both traditional and non-traditional roles determined more by physical capacity than gender, offers each partner opportunity and encouragement for growth. Most touching, perhaps, are the poems "Husband Cut My Hair" and "Serein/Rain from an Apparently Cloudless Sky," in which each in turn--threatened by serious illness--is supported without question by the other. These pieces are foreshadowed by the title poem, in which the phrase "grateful grief" captures a love so strong that, even while facing the possibility of its loss through death, the recipient can be grateful to have experienced it at all."

   - **Judy Hakola**, native rural New Englander, University of Maine Lecturer in English and community resource on Maine literature, especially Maine women writers.

"Patricia Ranzoni is a great storyteller. She will take you there."

   - **John Bear Mitchell**, Penobscot Nation, Wabanaki educator and storyteller.

LOVE POEMS FROM OUTBACK MAINE

Patricia Smith Ranzoni

We were crazy in those days of bedstraw and budding groves.

– Dana Wilde
"*Amateur Naturalist,*" *Bangor Daily News*

I noticed a bawdy, jolly, lusty, Elizabethan remnant now mixed with, but not thoroughly blended with, the Baptist code of conduct, which has been superimposed. The downeasters are not a colloid or a solvent into which the basics have lost their identity. One moment the lust comes out; the next moment it settles to the bottom of a crude mix and on top appears the righteous element.

– Dorothea Honora Moulton Balano
The Log of the Skipper's Wife

Oh, when the sun goes down,
I want to walk far out from town:
to walk with my love when the sun goes down,
to walk with my love far out from town.

– Philip Booth
"First Song" and *Pairs*

Bedding Vows

LOVE POEMS FROM OUTBACK MAINE

Copyright © 2012 by Patricia Smith Ranzoni
All rights reserved. No part of this book may be reproduced or transmitted in any form or by any means without written permission of the author. The acknowledgment pages constitute an extension of this copyright notice.

ISBN 978-1-943424-01-6

Library of Congress Control Number: 2015941218

The front cover photograph is of an original embroidered drawing by the author.

Back cover photograph by Ryan A. Newell.

Unity, Maine

for the love of heaven

Herein:

ઓ Lot One ભ

BEING DANCEY, DELICIOUS, NATURAL & REVERENT COVENANTS

GROWING UP HERE OR
    RESTING FIRST WITH THE WHAT IFS 12
SWAMP CAMP IN THE MORNING 13
from MAKING MAYBASKETS 14
FLASHBACK 19
A LITTLE ROMANCE 20
EATING OUT (HOW YOU GAVE YOURSELF AWAY) 21
LIMITED EDITION 22
WINTERS, WE REMEMBER GRASSING 23
DRESS CODE 24
HANCOCK COUNTY EVE 25
THAT OUR HOME SHALL BE FRAGRANT WITH LOAVES 26
GROUNDS (DESERVING OF EARTH) 28
FIRST SNOW 29
LABRADOR STAR 30
WE HUNT 31
MAKING POLENTA IN MAINE IN WINTER 32

BUCK NECK STEW   34
YOUR OLD & FOREVER WEDDING PATCHWORK   36
FIRE PLACES   37
ELEMENTS   38
FLOOD WATCH   40
ICEOUT/MAINE SEABOARD LOWLAND   41
HOLDING AND BEING HELD
   BY YOUR *LONG JOURNEY* ROBE   43
THE SPRING THAT COULDN'T COME   45
from ANOTHER LONG (22.)   46
ANNIVERSARY   47
NOTICE: NO HATEFUL PETITIONS ALLOWED   48
IN A MAINE VALLEY EVERY APRIL   49
WELL-SEASONED FARM WIFE COME SPRING   50
SWEETTALK   51
SWAPPING   52
GOOD LONG LOVES   53
ROSEMARY, HERB OF REMEMBRANCE   54
RIPENING LIKE EVERYTHING IN HIGH SUMMER   56
COCKEREL   57
ARTESIAN   58
CAPTAIN SNOWMAN'S GREAT GRANDDAUGHTER
    BUYS A MERMAID FOR HER BIRDBATH   59
SUMMER WOMAN   60
ANSWERING WHAT'S HE DOING TO HER, THE RAM   61

ANSWERING HOW COME YOU ALWAYS
   ROCK THE BABY   62
LATE   64
BEGINNING IN AUTUMN   65
HIS TIME   67
from PIANO LESSONS   68
from ANOTHER LONG (24.)   69
from ANOTHER LONG (47.)   70
FOR THE TURN OF THE CENTURY   71
MIXED-HEART MAINE   73
BY THE SOUND   75
from ANOTHER LONG (70.)   76
NO END TO IT   77
GLIMPSES   79
BEDDING VOWS   80

❧ Lot Two ☙

BEING CONSEQUENTIAL & EVERGREEN TESTAMENTS

HUSBAND CUT MY HAIR   82

SEREIN/RAIN FROM AN APPARENTLY CLOUDLESS SKY   83

UP THROUGH THIS FALLING DARK,
   A 70-STAR CONSTELLATION   91

POETRY AS WEDDING DRESS: WEDDING DRESS
   AS POETRY   93

ANSWERING WHAT MIGHT BE ECHOES
   OF AN OLD MALISEET SONG NOT MINE   100

Acknowledgments   101

The Author   105

ꙮ *Lot One* ꙮ

BEING DANCEY, DELICIOUS, NATURAL & REVERENT COVENANTS

lot:
being a matter for making a choice
to cast lots
the choice so made
what befalls one by lot
one's fortune in life
one's fate, destiny, portion
a number of associated people
a kind or type
the miscellaneous presented as one
a considerable amount
a piece of land with purpose
an allotment

One eventually comes to the plural / for safety in this state.

– John Marin

plant your seeds in a row
one for the pheasant
one for the crow
one to rot and one to grow

– old sowing chant

GROWING UP HERE
OR
RESTING FIRST WITH THE WHAT IFS

What if you were the boy riding his bike by to tread his uncle's hay?

What if it was at that farm I rode mine as far as?

What if after watering the cow by those great slurped pails drawn
       from the well out to the pasture where Daddy'd staked her
       for the day it was you invited me to jump in the just-in straw,
       you the boy laughing and falling into it with me, snapping
       the gatheringthread at the waistseam of my dress, tread-
       ing its hem with my grass-stained knees, field-dust glittering
       up that hug of setting sun through the mow window west
       shadowing daubed swallow nests all along the peak. You
       the one smelling all clover, and sweat
       beading your forehead and upper lip soft and first time sweet.
       And I liking it to the tune of allowing it
       meeting your kiss with one for you
       before jumping up and out of that confusing barn
       to pedal heart-pounding home in this new night, sure
       the whole family could see what I'd been up to
       the guilt I felt what did I know of guilt
       my *touched-his-shirt* hand over the inches of broken stitches
       I slip upstairs to mend from my 4-H kit.

What if you'd been that boy then
       would you have known you were lonely
       would I have seen sooner about poems?

SWAMP CAMP IN THE MORNING

Light seeps down from the mountain.
(*listennnn......listennnn....*)
Dawn, if it cared, or could see, could see
she has risen. (*hummming.......hummming.....*)

When she was a child and walked miles here
to swim in no one's cove, blisterfooted
and dirtskinned, she knew little beyond this skyline.

If someone were watching, seeing black hair
appear on the shore, they would have seen
how she hid herself even then.

Which isn't to say she didn't dream to someday
appear to a woodland love. No one told her
what she needed to know about roots and branches,
but growing up with frogs and turtles she knew
she belonged with their chants and screams
she'd someday hug over the water.

She can't get enough. Water lilies float
from her needles. Swamp roses an assignment
for her jellied mint.

from MAKING MAYBASKETS

CONTEXT: APRILS 1947 TO 1957, HANCOCK COUNTY, MAINE
(with remnants of songs, riddles, chants, and rhymes from
our schools and buses, churches, families, and outbacks)

(*Singing "There's Been a Change in Me" by Cy Coben.*)

You've saved small pasteboard containers all winter. Match-
boxes the size of the holder on the wall behind the stove.
Round Quaker Oats ones cut down. A sweetghosted box from chocolate
if you had one kept from Valentine's. The rooster running his prerogative 'round
'n' 'round the thawed yard his showy crow riding the bullish brook
chasing   kissing   chasing   kissing.

Your mother trades her eggmoney for pleats of tissue
and crinkled crepe paper at the 5 & 10 the colors of arbutus trailing
on the ledges where handsome young Lyman and Joannie Hutchins
from your mailman's family drive *head on . . .* exploding into those cliffs missing
the turn off the Waldo-Hancock Bridge where Bill Carpenter will someday come
to write and run, come to live and *breathe in* what people imagine you girls
imagine about those sailors off those tankers and barges come to load and unload.
Don't go down town there's a boat in come straight home there's a boat in
your father and mother and teachers warn lest you pick all Bucksport's rare wild
rose yarrow on the way to the wharf, encounter rainforest you don't know about
emotions, become women right there on the dock emerging with foreign flowers
between your souvenir breasts for the rest of your life.

> You don't know Robert Lowell is learning sailing
> and kissing a few miles downriver summers
> you don't know about, *classic summers* Elizabeth Bishop
> names it in North Haven poems.

Paper the color of shadblossoms you don't know roof and rug Ruth Moore's
writing place down back of her place in Tremont where you don't know
she's come home to claim her poems you don't know will someday seize, and kiss
your heart like an ancestor handing you something she wants to make sure
you get, the color of wild pear sprinkling your openair playhouse of fruit-crate
furniture and broken dishes from the farm and its antique dump in the woods
rainsmocked and flocked with pollens and insect wings, laced with webs,
feathers, salamander tracks and *remember this!*

Paper the color of forsythia you won't see
until your first trip out of state on this chartered bus
to Jack Wyrtzen's Youth for Christ Rally at Boston Garden,
returning with a bargainbible with leaves thin as spent narcissi
(you know from oldest farms) from answering the invitation
to come forward.
(sung) *Just as I am....I come, I come.*

        Not crocuses, snowdrops, hyacinths from bulbs
        you don't know about needing planting at closin'-in
        time, who'd *have* the time or money to spare, not for sale
        anywhere you've seen anyway you don't know anyone
        who actually has daffodils. But pussywillows, dandelions
        (a food not weed), skunk cabbage, maple and chokecherry
        flowers, fiddleheads, and

Paper the colors of those layers in your Grammie Dunbar's *what is it* riddle:
        Within a hall as white as milk,
        within a wall as soft as silk,
        within a fountain crystal clear,
        a golden apple doth appear.
        No doors there are to this stronghold
        yet thieves break in and steal the gold.

Paper the colors
of all the leaves in Jacob Buck valley!

Paper the tints of new growth nerving
against granite pinks old as earth.

You plan which little boxes will be which shades and designs.
Daffodil cups, lavender-trimmed rectangular ones. Which
fringed snowy and which for grass. Cones, and lantern ones
from cutting pastel tissue folded justright then unfolded
into lace, corners joinedup to a braided loop. Imagine Hattie Grindle's
paper parasols--miniature closed umbrellas
with candy in their creases. Anita, Barbara, Jean, known
for their stunningest--or--depending on your tongue--cunnin'est
kind.
        But doesn't Lowell make your mother's

        people's cemetery and our skunks famous (not the other
                                             way around
        the way your father's people wore skunkoil against the croup)
        seeing his own moonstruck eyes in theirs confessing his own
        wild taste for cultured trash? How Hancock County serves
        his genius these days freeing him to loosen and swivel his
        aesthetics no less, you may never be forgiven
        for proposing, than Elvis, and *shush*...
                                            what's this Howl!
        You've heard of Luzon and Mog Mog Island
        in the Philippines but don't know there's any such place
        as Brooklin Maine or Eggemoggin Reach except for the skit
        Mr. Mac has each 6th grade do called The Lighthouse
        Keeper's Daughter where the tallest boy gets to be the light
        so Bobby Terrill is yours and how you all split
        when Alfred Kettell like Barnacle Bill
(sung)   *Who's that knocking at my door...cries the fair young maiden.*
        It's only me from over the sea, I'm Barnacle Bill the sailor
        chases Judith Cropley you don't know will die so young
        losing her leg, 'round and 'round Bob you don't know
        will die so young working maintenance at the mill
        no connection they'll say. Gangly he stands while all roar
        in the gym but you'll hardly be able to smile
        his last reunion his face turning back into that light
        he's leaving on and *Dear Christ*
        you hope you kissed him goodbye.
    This is the forest primeval you memorize with voice sad
        (and not unprophetic) for Rena Grey in 7th or 8th and
  ...he tapped with his whip on the shutters, but all was locked
and barred;/He whistled a tune to the window,/and who
should be waiting there.../.../.../ Plaiting a dark red love-knot
into her long black hair.

You cut across wrinkles of your women's art the way you've been taught
playing sepalous garlands and corolla strings like paper dolls, pressing petals
and leaves out round with your thumbs.
You make boiled flour-and-water paste.

        You don't know E.B. these years calls the management
        of his desk paste a # one problem.
        You don't know George Oppen is pasting words
        over words (because neither he nor Mary type) but loosely

so they can be tried and untried
like where to stick the right bud and leaf on what handle
or ruffle, floating discrete words over Penobscot waters you
don't know about from their island-bobbing boat. You
don't know you are learning alliteration from wagons
on depths just as capable of drowning. Not the rhythm
of trimming sails exactly but *build that load, walk that hay,*
trimming, trimming, your father's chants teaching you *that*
ballet where to tread to an edge to balance and not fall off,
your own sweat your own salt, chaff
an inland sting and after full days after days of it not
foxtrots you don't know about over any harbor
you don't know about but The Barbara Polka, the *schottische*,
and Irene Goodnight at the Gypsy or up to the hall, spitcurls
on your cheeks, blackest ponytail the Methodist minister
calls a sin down to your waist swingin' in squares and rounds,
not chintz and linen you don't know about but cotton broomstick
skirts (you don't even need a pattern for) twirling
over net petticoats starched in sugarwater dripped outside to dry
so stiff they scrunch like iceout from the racing brook
that spicy old scent of life wanting to chase and kiss itself.

So you turn out Maybaskets for the Willis kids
and Johnsons and Conners and Smiths. Allisons, Bridges, Grindles
and Hurds. Winchesters, Gowans and Whites planning which for which
keeping the old promise to chase and kiss
and always give the new
people the best.

Last of April you make the fill. Your mother's divinity, sister's
peanut butter, your
cocoa fudge keeping the old secrets of the full rolling boil
to the soft ball stage you keep testing for
with drops in cups of cold water
'til the syrup gathers in your fingertips
like a nipple at rest
then waiting, waiting, to let it cool
before beating out its shine
having waxed paper to turn onto that *instant* it sets.

May First it goes like this: you've picked through dreams
through days and nights where

you'll deliver, which
heart where, not by moonlight

        but after school after supper after chores before dark.
        After rings on the still-party line all agreeing to fake,
        listening for who'll be home when. *I'll come to thee* [before]
        moonlight, though hell should bar the way.

Across the valley youngsters watch who's where, when.
Baskets behind their backs, they walk or bike
to each house, those inside pretending not to notice.
Not since Una Wardwell's day when from eggshells
fancied with wallpaper have most Maybaskets
been light or right enough to hang from knobs, so you nest
them on granite and wooden steps quiet as birds
setting down. *Knock* and *run!*   Cheeks flushed to russets,
you *chase*   *kiss*   *chase*   *kiss*   *remember this!*

FLASHBACK

softness from dialing the phone

like lifting the lid to my music box

A LITTLE ROMANCE

denim
dimity

organza

EATING OUT
(How You Gave Yourself Away)

How, waiting for me,
you balanced your fork
in your Michelangelo hand
as if still savoring the spice
while I *mmm*ed my last
elegant swallows.

And how, if our misguided
waitpeople, noting the afterglow
from your empty dish, interrupted
with their eager-to-please
May I take your plate? you fully
forgave with *No thank you,
I'll wait for her*, showing
I'd never have to finish alone.

LIMITED EDITION

When I gave you
my schedule
so you'd know
where I'd be,
you covered your heart
with your hands
(and mine with love)
and said you know
where I am.
Now I know
what a Valentine is.

WINTERS, WE REMEMBER GRASSING

drawn to each other's faces and scents,
(hair and teeth you said) hands and feel,
sounds, and ways of being,

        found,

having kissed and pressed, guessed
in sweet trust up and down the countryside,
our beings choosing,

        (*What were the chances*, you.
         Was it longing, I.
         Yes, a forlorn lovesickness, you.)

we cast our lots together becoming singular
thereunto plighting our truth

in ignorance and innocence knowing naught
beyond our far wooded and watered childhoods,

once located and recognized we said we would,
native grasses our witnesses,
        wild strawberry sod our bed

DRESS CODE

in the back pasture
        where
            barely adequate fences
            delineate expectations
is bare
in pinespilled cloth

whatever fur
one wears to the sun
is fine

cow eyes wear us
        swimming in high summer selves
well-bred women gathering
for our mounting gifts
        brimming and considerate
their dreamy watch showing
we know how to behave here
        all tongue and drool

        all graze and cream

HANCOCK COUNTY EVE

                hayfields
                hedgerows
                edgelife
    jungle
    the farm
    the pond throbs

fire
flies

three spent men give in
to a porch

                grandfather
                his son
                his
2 beers and a fudgsicle

the valley fills and smells
        with muggy night

in upstairs chambers
    a woman peels
        windows open
            to honeysuckle
                conclusions

THAT OUR HOME SHALL BE FRAGRANT WITH LOAVES

Keep the chainsaw sharp, good man,
                        and I will make your bread.

Keep the tractor popping along
                        and I will make your bread.

Keep the woodsroad open, sir,
                        and I will make your bread.

Keep the trailer ready to haul
                        and I will make your bread.

We'll keep the woodshed stacked and dry
                        and I will make your bread.

Keep the chopping stump propped, my dear,
                        and I will make your bread.

Keep the axe head honed and true
                        and I will make your bread.

We'll keep the woodbox loud with logs
                        and I will make your bread.

We'll keep the woodstove stoked, my mate,
                        and I will make your bread.

We'll keep the flour bin heaped and grained
                        and I will make your bread.

I'll keep the staples stocked, my sweet,
                        keep the yeast jar fed,

keep coming home and keeping us warm
                         in trouble and *wellth* as we live long.

Keep these vows with me, my love,
                         and to the end I will make your bread.

GROUNDS
(Deserving of earth)

the black-capped nation
has returned
from summer woods
to the pasture's flushing edge

bees are nursing aster blues
thistle purples
and night-chewed drops
where they brown

each patch
its own essential smell
the body it is
what we've let go

oh the inner insect thrums
and chimes oh

I could live out here forever
without a house
being my ancestor
grandmother

mother   sister   girl
dance with me
my mate
do you smell

this scarlet vine
of a gown is that you
using the poplars
to applaud

FIRST SNOW

for the divorcing

And isn't it true:
what didn't get done
doesn't matter anymore. Buried.
That's all she wrote your grandfather
would say about things being over. Some
things can't be saved. Uncle George says

the doe seen crossing has twins,
says she comes regularly by the barn.
He's seen her rear up on hind legs,
hoof the air, her fawns following,
learning whatever it is she's teaching.
What *National Geographic* would give
to have that if only he could've gotten it
on film. Imprints

of all our winters expose an annual ache
for what we can't name but are pulled by.
To windows. To fields. To woods.
To remembered good and grief. The truth
of seasons, what it means: something else
ending. *Rise up to the cold. Sense for signs.
The way to go. Your instinct for spring.*

LABRADOR STAR
(*old mitten pattern*)

Your hands have no doubt grown
a good deal since I measured them
from the base of your palm
to the fingernail of your ring finger
to figure where to begin to decrease;
my own art, now that it's my turn,
plotted out over small squares.

Yours were the handsomest and
hardest mittens I ever made.
How could we know the entangle-
ments of divorce might mean
I might not see you again? Oh save
those mittens knit years ago,
my love carried untangled behind
their starry design handed down,
the bright white strand
in that navy sky.

WE HUNT

> *from before there were stores*
> *then money*
> *to keep our place in the balance of things*
> *to refuse spiritless food*

In glassed grass he stands alert on the ridge,

rifle gentled in ancient work.

Heart kind as any killing our kind with words.

> Good men and women out here hunt
>
> that we may go on. That the land we tend
>
> tends us that we may provide for our own.

Snow knows his motives so do deer sensing

him a worthy one to be taken by or elude.

MAKING POLENTA IN MAINE IN WINTER

per ogni zia, zio, e cugino / for each aunt, uncle, and cousin

The Atlantic Queen is ready, radiating her distinctive heat.
He has seen to it, woodbox brimming with its mix of quick
and slow burning sticks, before setting out with the men to track
this winter's food. She is deft at native fry bread, journey cakes,
corn bread, anadama, Indian pudding and steamed brown but cornmeal
cooked this way is foreign and she's had to learn.

She takes down the good pan, dented and stained, and draws
the coldest water from deep in the well. Her fingers find the right
wooden spoon with its edge straight for keeping the bottom scraped
and lumps from forming.

The stoked stove rules the cooking room, telling the water when
to boil, inviting the salt and stone ground grain--half coarse, half fine.
She knows hands are called for to drift it in a slow stream into the roil
thickening not unlike a dream.

The spoon must not linger any more than the old country fire
can be allowed to die down. Her job, she knows, reminding
her of the constancy she's heard was required in the endless tending
of their fired charcoal mounds in the Berkshires when they arrived,
that they not be spoiled.

The ways have been brought over and up to now and the woman
wants the house's smell to be thought. The men will be watching
for the light at the window from farther than anyone knows.

The aunts and cousins showed her how to tell when it's done.
The spoon must be able to stand alone and the stirring is constant
and long and scorching but the mixture grows firm as their histories,
ready for the cheese and platter warming on the back of the range.

The woman's face is red as the men's, frostbit and starved as bears trudging home. They lean aside their guns and kiss her.
The aura about them is dense with ethnic honor, these evergreen men.

The polenta feeds and warms them as nothing else can.

BUCK NECK STEW

for the winter solstice

Everything in it from Ed and God though belief is not required for potatoes and carrots to swell. Onions, tomatoes, garlic, beans. Reverent fingers in the soil and hunt. Fire from the wood from the land from his hands.

The Paul Winter Consort's Silver Concert on the radio. Gabriel's ashwork dancing in my arms, lid off to collect the wolf and human howls around the fire and stew. Gal's prayers.

This summer at our place, he saw the old gathering basket, nearly worn out, and sat with it, listening, eyeing and feeling, honoring his wife's knowing gaze. Lifted and held by him it rejoiced to his touch, remembering its source.

They took it back, home to his tree-pounding place where it would board with them upriver, the way my family did years ago, rooted in relative time.
And when it was soundly born again, they delivered it in the shortest days of longest nights, surprising us where people gather at the book place at the mouth of the river for stories and songs, candles and cake. The gift of myself back to myself when he laid it in my arms, his heart and his wife's heart overweaving. When I raised its new lid it filled with our sighs and praise.

After the basket had gathered that night's thousands-of-years-old-fears that the sun would leave forever, along with promises to light, without waste, our houses and trees, and build fires and listen to one another's hopes--*and help*--if it will please come back; and we had waved them back upriver with kisses, I brought it home to sleep with me and my old man, listening for reasons.

Every longest night since, rehearing the strains, I lift it to dance, opening it to give and receive the whole world singing and promising on the airwaves, praying for Reason, which is to say Light, to return.

I twirl with it, and bow, and the basket lifts me with reinforced legs, refurbished ribs, arms renewed, and thick sweetgrass rim which is to say dream. Stronger. All the more useful, we are grandmother and grandfather vessels restored with felt respect. As with the venison stew, my good husband's sacramental voice. God food.

This stew and its story is what we've brought north to my birthplace to join our appeals with yours and all of ours to the Earth's.

YOUR OLD & FOREVER WEDDING PATCHWORK

a triolet

Here, dears, a runner for your *unity* flame
pieced from our hope chests, Indian baskets, hearts,
for yours. The way we save for rites in our name –
here, dear, a runner for your *unity* flame.
Joined ribbon, lace, crocheted, embroidered and sewn,
from your grandmother's and great aunts' homestead arts –
here, dears, a runner for your *unity* flame,
pieced from our hope chests. Indian baskets. Hearts.

FIRE PLACES

> *It stays exciting to see the stone.*
> – Jeff Gammelin
> "Moraine Maker"

Maple flavored flames flicker
on slate then under shelves
of Gammelin-spirited rock. Again

on old ceiling pine. And again!
In ancestral gold on your chest
rising and falling in the glow.

A Roman silhouette as definite,
strong, as the granite lines
I see you against. In your arms

I hold the ages in this now,
this ancient and forever time.
Sacraments of heartfires

and happinesses make this
snowed in day a worshipful thing.
When we wake

you bring Catani's antique ice
fishing tip-ups in from the shed
resurrecting them with reverence

on the altar that is hearth
to receive their own blessing,
their own memoried grace.

ELEMENTS

Lines down. Winter's turn.

You've cut, hauled, split
the wood for our marooned fire
up night after night both of us
keeping the pipes from freezing.
Our one warm room fragrant
with kindling and lichened logs.

I bring in my petite boudoir chair
with curved rockers needing me
and peach velvet tufts some lady
would never guess would end
oh begin at a Searsport sale
and show you how dancey
it helps me be
here by the hearth
in my long night's gown
oh let me fold you in.

I wish for the lights never
to come back on. For darkness
to come in its own good time
and take as long as it needs.
What shine and warmth there is,
up to us. As here, now,
this candle quivering its flirty skirt
oh let me undance your shirt
these drafts just piano shivers
I've taught myself to play.

*Humming....*our stove
can't contain the flames
we take turns stoking in its belly.

Last traces of melting ice sizzle
from the cherry and maple,
water boiling over its kettle
oh let's bathe in this flickering power
configuring on the ceiling
this petaled oil I've pressed and saved
for us this wine you've found.

*Oh stay and listen by this fire with me
burning* oh give yourself to your life
let me be your wife until our shadows
die down into morning.

FLOOD WATCH

What can I do but build a small blaze....
        – Paulann Petersen
           "Be Here When I Can See You, When I Can't"

    At last it isn't snow. Still, too wintry
to go back to sleeping in their unheated upstairs
quite yet. Up before daylight, shivering, she
builds the fire across the pelted room stoking
hardwood pallets he sawed before his operation
to see them through now the woodpile's gone.
Flickers under the stove door cast a thin dawn.
Soon their breakfast water will boil and call
through their covers above the driving rain.
Winds within the stove and outside make one roar.
Sparks surround and entrance them with their own
old sounds. Through sashes to the east she watches
what she heard in the dark--*day*--breaking wide,
cold to the bone, and wetter than wet out.
Wild trees and bushes swim and thrash
all the way down the field over his mountain
of a shoulder, last of night silhouette, swelling
then sinking into the panes.

ICEOUT/MAINE SEABOARD LOWLAND

first quarter moon, April

bringing me my dream
to live atop the tallest pine on the point

to swoop and dive through aerial acrobatics
our courting is known for

to grab one another's bills, preen
one another's blackness
and coo for life, complex, as noted

to have labored together to weave our platform nest
from hundreds of flights collecting shine
from all the firesites on the shore

to have for a neighbor the turtle mother
who gives us her hair
the one who, hearing the turtles' screams,
shames the poachers away
the black market ones from away
netting in shifts destroying balance

to know the truth about wilderness,
desolation, scavenge, hunt
about leaving
about food others don't know is food

how to disappear for protection

to have a low raspy voice all hear over the water
but not all can identify but one man held so dear
he named his swamp camp for it, the wetlands-one,
and the whistling man and his wife and children

and theirs promising to protect

to have the capacity to imitate human speech
to speak with such rhythms and codes
observable things happen
for instance young ones answer
to feel such patterns out my mouth
to hear the silence between each croak
to cause people to hush, cock their heads to get

to be such an indicator Noah
would have sent you out with the dove

to seek the cool depths of the forest come summer

to be missed

to soar flat-out free

      to be called *wolfbird*

            to be known as *raven*

HOLDING AND BEING HELD
BY YOUR *LONG JOURNEY* ROBE
(From Siletz Back Home to the Other Side)

for Lisa and Kendall

Waking from our cross-continental migration,
with your Pendleton "Spirit of the Salmon" blanket
washing over us, as we imagine *alevin*, I feel its deep
and sky blues gulping its bled red sundown waves
floating us together. The way you said the Yachats
meets the Pacific. Fresh joining salt. Place of healing
to your people. Two of your mighty fish leap as one
up our grateful bed, their aura curves a sacred mist
finning our long passage together before the end.
Life beyond love to guide if not protect us
the rest of the dangerous way.

In our yard the gravel and mud are heaving
into peaks from frost thrusts as if our own
mountain range might erupt and spill lava
some future dirt worker might find--black
and rock hard, encasing spruce and hemlock boughs
and last year's cones pocking the drive--shin high,
petrified around age-old sticks and stones
miniature-looking after your ancient flow, thick,
down Tillicum Beach.

Still seven feet of snow up north they say.
Deer and moose *just skin and bones* desperate
by the roads for the least bare sprig.
How can I tell you how ready we are for spring
how far this is from the greens along your rainy rim?

We shall wrap ourselves against this Atlantic cold
in the milled wool of your Chinook gift I'll stitch

with your names, your smoked elk in our cells,
preserving visions of your home, tribal warm,
in the rivery chambers of our hearts
'til our seven-foot *bonnefire* outside, and our house-
heating hearth flames in, jump down to fossil-long
memory of us meeting, countless migrations ago.

THE SPRING THAT COULDN'T COME

grief,
all was grief
and war

until a splendid skunk stink
up through the front room floor

shocking shoots under the pear

a peace-filled man's vernal desire

from ANOTHER LONG (22.)

he brings her
a long-stemmed heart
sized sun, sensing
her longing
for some
small
petalous
shine

ANNIVERSARY

This morning
        we stood, arms knit,
                watching swallows flirt

beyond the glass
        and I swear,
                watching us, they

might be saying
        in swallow conjugation
                the same as we:

look,
        dear,
                what an exciting pair!

NOTICE: NO HATEFUL PETITIONS ALLOWED

for our door
for EqualityMaine

Nancy and Flo, David and John, Mary Jane and Sue
spoken here. Our fire is their fire. Our food their food.
Our beds their beds.

Can't you find some loving work to do
                       in this wounded, wounding world?

Stop right there, please.
                       Your deed is not welcome here.

IN A MAINE VALLEY EVERY APRIL

Trout's what a good man brings his good wife
come spring. Alders showing when, sprouting mice ears
along each branch, tight ice finally gone. Fishing,
he catches his dear's doubting face the itinerant poet
called wonderful wondering if she remembers he's
told her too, thinking how many winters they've
weathered together to come again to the banks of another
spring. She's reviewing the same thing on her knees
in renewing green, knifing damp dirt for taproots
to slice whole dandelion knots for her colander pile
when he, whistling, comes with them gutted and laced
on a whittled shoot. She fires the spider cast-iron hot
with sizzling butter then when the lemon and melon spots
have crusted brown with flavored flour and those tail M's
curled crisp she swirls that mess of greens to wilt
in that taste until those brookies are cooked through
but not too. Spread whole, soft bones and all,
onto palms of her best oat, they bite into the grounds
they haven't left to live instead some other place
doing their damnedest to overpower the sorrow bread
all this way from Waco and Oklahoma City.

WELL SEASONED FARM WIFE COME SPRING

Humming, "When You Say Nothing At All"
                – Country song, words by
                   Paul Overstreet and Don Schlitz

Up before him her work begins. Quiet letters
stocked with *Aunt Muriel's had a stroke,*
you should see cousin Wallace's garden,
Jeannie's moving, thanks for the card, and
what recipe do you want for the kids' wedding
while the wash soaks, breakfast smells
wending upstairs to twitch awake his day.
Dandelion flowers to pick midst blackfly swarms,
douse with boiling water set for wine
wash on the line. Rugs to shake floors to mop
he's long gone to the back pasture
where he loves best to be.

Knots a cotton napkin with hermits hot from the oven
into a migrant's sack. Pours a jar coldest milk.
Sets out without shoes, habit driven,
across the yard where chicks test mothers ducking
through their magic cedar arch. Robins soar before her
where they'll play *bocce* with the children
come summer if she can get him to stop.
Down the pondwalk, along the dam listening
for his tractor's *puttputtputt* where he'll be pulling
old barbed wire out of the ground.

Sometimes she wishes he'd talk to her more.
Spreads her skirt in the wild strawberry blossoms,
violets, cinquefoil, in the concentrated sun in front
of the huge tire sheltering them from gusts off the ledge.
He savors the fruit in her still warm spicecakes, her milk
hitting the spot. She adores his white mustache,
soiled hands. He wasn't expecting this not even noon.

SWEETTALK

Hold your hammer, honey, your board,
your wood hauled from the lot
for Harry Woodman's saw.
Back from the field, honey, and look what I've got!
Smell my fingers, honey, and look at my full bowl!
That tickles licking my fingers, honey,
ain't this some great luck? Pine. Fruit. Fine pickin's
don't you think, honey?

SWAPPING
OR
WHY I LOVE GROWING OLD OUT BACK

because when my old man
finished closing in the new shed
and called me to come see
we looked at each other and giggled
and he said he'd give me
a couple strawberries if I would
I lifted my skirt
and we laughed like hell

GOOD LONG LOVES

remember this come winter
when the vines are remembering themselves

new barn peaks all pine-y

aura of the quarter moon
still ours as much as any's

bullfrogs up from the pond
swimming in our thighs

ROSEMARY, HERB OF REMEMBRANCE
L'Erba Di Memoria

birthday tribute turned elegy for Howard's love, Rosemary Augello Bridges (1922-2008)

What did we know of Rosemary over on the Town Farm Road
where none had grown before but that she was colorful as
the Mediterranean lands our father told us about after the war?
And that was so far, we could only imagine something that

sun-loving over in our valley where everything was winter
and getting ready for winter. We only knew about the glamour
she gave us glimpses of in *impetuosi* eyes and *rosso* lipstick.
And don't I recall *bella* dresses, *elaborati* heels and *trasparenti*

stockings? Looking back, I wonder if she could even find olive oil
at the A & P downtown and what else she missed growing wild
from her distant home. I wish I had lived closer to observe
and help preserve her different ways but we were only allowed

to walk and ride our bikes so far and had to settle for peeks
from the school bus and special occasions. Our cupboards
were mixed blood Yankee native and plain, what grew outside
our doors and in our woods. And once in great whiles lemons

when they could be afforded for pie. If we had only known
to rub them together with pine we'd have had our own hint
of the "sovereign oil" we find rosemary's is called. Scrumptious
scent, highly aromatic evergreen, even curative, who wouldn't

prize that for a name? With the power to bring couples together
by its touch, a sprig pressed into bridal wreaths and bouquets.
Pungent, tucked behind an ear to aid the concentration of scholars.
Exchanged between friends to signify loyalty.

Tossed into the graves of departed loves, even buried
with the pharaohs, burned in sick rooms to disinfect, believed

to have powers to banish evil. All hearsay, yes?
But I'm telling you I believe that part about gypsies seeking it

to rinse their dark hair because I bet she did, hers so *gloria*-black
and wouldn't we all drop everything and go on a rosemary hunt
right now to restore our own locks? Gypsy, yes, she charmed
like a gypsy and I should know, spying that *bella signora*

through the years. And I confess, once having my own taste
of Mediterranean spice, to adding rosemary to my store,
growing it for every delectable dish earning my Italian, rubbing it between my fingers, breathing in its fragrance along the way.

Marrying it with orris root in potpourri and perfume recipes.
But should I feel contrite, or pleased, to have failed to maintain
a plot as it is written in herbals how it grows particularly well
in gardens tended by strong-willed women? I leave that to you,

Rosemary. But I shall try harder now to cultivate those two
petite seeds in each flower, aspects of you we can attest
are especially attractive to bees, legend (always a delight to see)
having it they go by the names *Charlotte* and *Stephanie*.

RIPENING LIKE EVERYTHING IN HIGH SUMMER

His sweet sweaty teeshirt, bent and rounded in the field,

    moves rhythmically across the ledge

        the way a silvering bear might browse.

Patch to patch I watch from his potato rows

    in love with him parting the daisies,

        buttercups, and vetch for strawberries wild

and juicy as we've stayed in our devotion.

COCKEREL

          young man
you must not
think of me
in fertile terms
except as we both
love languages for love
must not
think of me
as the riper chick
to favor for your
volcanic quakes
I'm a plump old biddy
foolish for a cock
spouting his best
doodle-doo   come
when you'd like
I'd applaud yours of course
but best roost right there
lest my chanticleer hear
then even if you fly
by the book with luck
you'll only be chased
to the brook not
lose an eye *cluck cluck*
when he struts his talons high
brings his wings down
s t r e t c h e s
his gorgeous iridescent neck
to my direction
you must know
he's got me
by his crow and crown

cluck   cluck

ARTESIAN

when you
      showed me
the foot valve
      you'd had
to replace
      in the well
I adored it
    like the first
time I saw you
     its purpose-
ful parts private
      and oh so
handsome
    the only way
to bring up water
     I couldn't
let you throw
       it away

CAPTAIN SNOWMAN'S GREAT GRAND-
DAUGHTER BUYS A MERMAID
FOR HER BIRDBATH

Because he commanded her DNA out of Bucksport aboard the schooner *N.E. Symonds* to Cayenne, French Guiana, in the Caribbean trade.

Because family both sides came by sea and live from it to this day.

Because her father was United States Navy on the Atlantic, Pacific, Mediterranean, China, and Philippine Seas aboard the *U.S.S. Uhlmann* for the signing in Tokyo Bay.

Because of his King Neptune initiation certificate for crossing the Equator and his anchor and heart tattoos she and his other children begged to see.

Because the Portuguese-Maine woman, of New Bedford's "dead whale or a stove boat" possibility, had it for sale in her Bar Harbor shop.

Because she heard its cast iron siren song across the waves of spruced and gussied trove, and longed to fetch it home to their daisy-frothed main.

Because she has the perfect crow's nest propped atop coastal stone, a galley-size tidal bowl reflecting celestial mariner maps.

Because as she balances, all 12 inches of herself, on her vessel's gunnel facing East, her head resting back into the net her fingers knit behind her, her breasts buoyant under her floating hair, she catches dawn and dew with the scales of her glistening body fishtailing over the whitecap peonies splashing above the kelp mulch, at peace, it appears, home in rain.

Because her swarthy mate with an Ellis Island chantey of his own deserves a beneficent mermaid swimming through his work, his land-bound hands missing the olive air salted by the Ligurian, Tyrrhenian and Adriatic, still imagining the *S.S. LaGascogne* oceaning Pasquale and Rosalinda all this way. All this time. A cellular current she'll ride jubilantly with him.

SUMMER WOMAN

Rugosa days. Wine-splashed magenta to mauve.
Pink glories vining wild on the shore, she returns
to a salt-slope house she's given over to pastels.
Her feminine taste allowed full shrift now he's gone.
Just like that she snaps her fingers to company guessing
him in family shots on the refrigerator door *just*

like that. Met off at school. Drove that 1951
Chevy convertible all the way to Maine to court her in,
settling in Fresno. Now he's gone, summers she
comes home, softening her 1800s cape with petal tints.
In new wood floors, the lift of light grain. Bouquet-
stained bower overlooking the tides, Vaughn

and Judy's lobster boat, John Small Cove, clear across
Sorrento to Mount Desert where she takes morning coffee
and evening Napa Valley *blanc.* Plays piano and sings
bringing up the 30s and 40s for lucky ones who leave
with her flair and interest like pollen all over them
sensing deeply how they, too, might fruit.

Gathers crab-dip and crackers back to the kitchen
where he's waiting his turn where he'll breathe her in
the way she remembers and in a heart-stopping pain
she'll know again the garden he showed her she was
and because they are true, all these swears-she-hears-hims,
she won't make her bed but to change it.

Over Flander's Bay the whole old sky becomes
a breathstopping rose the way good long loves do.

ANSWERING WHAT'S HE DOING TO HER, THE RAM

vignette: scene to fit on a vine leaf

Fall in the pasture air
                      his flaring nostrils
                                        her standing readiness

Children at the barnyard window asking.

Oh, they're breeding, dear (taking the sacred chance).
That's how their lambs are made. How babies are made.

        Even people?

Even people.

        You mean Daddy did that to you?

Yes, dear, only we call it *making love*.

        You mean Daddy did that to you three times?

grape leaves
        on his cedar log frame
                            whispering Earth's ways

ANSWERING HOW COME YOU ALWAYS ROCK THE BABY

Because I read him a poem through your mama's skin about coming out
> when he was still in her baby-growing place

because I was happy when I heard he was coming and I'm glad he's here
> like you.

Because I paced, too, waiting and wanting him born.
Because I held him minutes in the world and whenever I could after
because I'm his grandmother and want him to know what I feel like
> and sound like and smell like so he'll know me the way I know
> him.

Because he rocked in warm water in your mama's womb and misses it
> and because she likes to rock him, too, and I can help.

Because for more hundreds of thousands and thousands of hundreds
> of years
> > than we can count, people have liked rocking children so much
> > they have made all kinds of wonderish roundish carriers to rock
> > them in. You know: cradles and swings and animal seats
> > with springs,
> > back and forth chairs and to and fro toys that tip and then
> > come back
> > again (*See-saw, Margery Daw...*)

Because I have a lap and arms and a chair on rockers, see how it's made.
Because rocking's what we're supposed to do with babies
because all creatures of the earth who know enough curl around their new
> ones and cuddle them with safe sounds like *urrrr* and *umf umf umf*
> and *kooooo* and whatever sounds they make to mean: you
> are our baby and we love you.

Because hearing *loo loo loo lye* and *la la la lay* he'll hear how sounds
> make meanings and like to hear *lily*, and other flower names and
> *linger*, which means stay awhile and he might, and *Lilliputian*
> meaning very small things he might want stories about.

Because my mama and daddy taught me rocking songs their
> mamas and daddies taught them like *Too-ra-loo-ra-loo-ral...* and
> *I had a little doggy that used to sit and beg...* and

because we want to teach new children in our family
    so you will teach yours.
Because I gave birth to his father and sang these lullabies to him and
because rocking his baby's like rocking him again.
Because I sang these songs to you when I met you and you were two and
because I would have rocked you when you were a baby if you
    were in our family then and
because I would rock you any time you want me to now
because the time you little ones want to be rocked is so short isn't it.
Because no matter how old we get a few rocks a day help keep the blues
    away;
because even when we're grown we like to hold, *la la lee,*
    and be held, *la la lye,* and remember how like a lullaby
    it feels to move in someone's arms like Grampa holds me,
    and we sway, *la la lay!* in our own rocking way,
    and call it dancing.

LATE

Night
in Maine and between wet
whispers August gusts pelt
           this dry old place
with dangerously
needed rain.

Pine sprays
and cedar hands
scrub summer's dust
    from what clapboards they
with this wind
can wash.

Safe with my
love in this relief
I think how we grown
   from this glacier-gouged clay
have been cut so deep.
How living by rock

has marked
and petrified us
to hurt. How line by line
           deed by deed
here we sleep or don't
in one hard bed

the nearer our ends
the more or less we cry.

BEGINNING IN AUTUMN

Valley air still warm enough to hedge, he
spends the day bush-hogging the back edge
of the grown-in field instead of bringing in
with her last flowers and herbs they dare
stay out longer.

It is Saturday night he bathes and shaves.
It is the full moon she bathes and shines.

He drives her over to Verona Island
to Wood's take-out for what may well be
their last haddock sandwich of the century.

It is the eve of another life. He is done
working away and is coming home
to the place he'll never stop thanking her
for bringing him.

They look to one another through same
young eyes and drive back to Bucksport
to the new town dock.

Across the river the fort is lit, as if now
that the battle is over, when there never was
one, it's time to admire night as well as day
what an astonishing thing to have lasted
and been saved.

Turning on Celtic strings on the radio,
windows down, they step out
into their brand new lot and swing
into their good fit, re-feeling their first dance
upriver at a university thing not knowing
what hit them.

Alone, and together, at the mouth of this inside tide, they run on far-off strains,
amassed bands of the spheres, seeing
themselves nothing but quick notes floating in the airs over the bay they are ready
for whatever comes next. The outback moon
pipes them home, harvesty as they.

September's elder light intensifies and burns
through their upstairs sash becoming
a *Night Watch* tartan, restoring worn wood
and walls, inventing a bolt of lunar plaid.

HIS TIME

His birthday she rises early to start the beans soaked all night.
So long since they've kept the ritual of Saturday baked-all-day beans.
Picked over. Rinsed. Bought from Floyd's annual Aroostook run.
400 pounds this year from some farmer still doin' it the old way.
Come fall their stable heights stacked with drying stalks, roots up,
shells spiraling into grins as if they might know what blueribbon suppers
and breakfasts and lunches they store. She remembers flailing them
in a grainbag over a cloth on Dunc's plank floor to thresh
like scrumptious secrets too good to be kept.
Up earlier himself, hard-*at* storm windows, she works to his whistles

which through their time have become the necessary ingredient.
Beans parboiled until their skins crack and curl when blown on and she
smiles back, adding a couple apples for special from the tree by his tool-
shed, ripened too, by the tunes he shapes his breath into with lips hers
have adored. She picks from their winter supply drying onions he grew,
put by in their net sacks. Salt pork slab--he didn't--she saws
into a fat comb. Not since cutting down farming for work in town.
Maybe, he sometimes says, testing how it sounds, *maybe when I retire*
may be they will, once more, so the grandchildren can know. Grow
everything they need beginning again with a family cow maybe from an ad

in *Uncle Henry's* the notion keeping them going.
Brown sugar, molasses, mustard, pepper and salt. All day. The kids
will come. Return him knowledge of what he's given.
She'll open her first jars this season's pickles and test all day the yeast-
dough knowing each stirring-down is required for it to rise,
then rise, *then rise* to its highest a marriage alive and oh the house
smelling so good of its hardmade bread. The greatgrandmother
invited to the piano to play by ear old songs the little ones dance by the fire
to with aunts and uncles, memories they'll hold on their tongues
elegant like a spoon of beans she takes him to taste at noon.

from PIANO LESSONS

To open a piano is to open a door. Or close one.

Once a child has truly entered the piano the piano has found her.
pp *For life.*

So that when a woman, grown, climbs out of the pond,
out of the grey clay dripping with the medicine of muskrat water,
and the astonished October moon is her kind of note, she will turn
to the First Movement of the *Sonata quasi una Fantasia*
and play the moonlight like an old mate, new, in the **adagio** dark.

from ANOTHER LONG (24.)

When her legs can't read the literature of walk, he lifts and pushes
and holds her along.

When her speech scrabbles like dropped letters mixed on an
illiterate floor, he turns to her

with strewn emotions as to a shattering next chapter he's devoted
to helping her discover.

When her whole body writes itself into alien alphabets twisting
its tongue with torsion drive,

he finds her face, tenders her hair back to an untangled place,
and kisses her to a dream.

from ANOTHER LONG (47.)

(*Dreaming company...*)

come visit by my bed
bringing pages you've composed or admire
given in your truest reading voice even
when my lids clamp closed I'll hear

no need to stage it
with performance others
might applaud or prize gestures
my eyes can't open to

your sound close
and individual to cotton me
around and away on
or for a comfort in which I might stay

FOR THE TURN OF THE CENTURY

Her bread is made. Her pies. Everything roasting or simmering
on back burners what doesn't need to be kept cold. The wood-Queen's
fiery *snap-to* put to her proper use serving a house trying to hold its own.

The woman worn from another year's work trying to save the farm,
steps out to take a breather in air quiet enough to hear the brook
she's come to require, times like this, to cool her stove-hot skin.

Over the field she hears it the way she always does, needing only
to open to it any day or night of her life. She's been pledged to it, and it
to her, from when she was a girl and it showed her her will.

The last Thanksgiving of the nineteen hundreds, here, inland
from the coast of Maine, is a contrary one. The ground is not frozen and
as if not sure of North, it's been warm enough for the lilacs to green as if

unable to wait for May. The bulbs' long dark won't be as long and dark
this year, if the deep frost ever comes. But unless it does, nothing
will keep, and if she's to make it through the rest she must

get off her feet. There's a while yet before the family is due and they'll
understand her time out. They might not even know, if she's up and at it
again before they arrive. She leaves the door open

to her husband's lullaby, his going about *his* part
between stints hunting on the edges between pasture and woods.
She leaves the door open so she can hear him whistling each time

he returns and he can hear her hum and smell the smell of home.
Her eyelids fall. Her breath. In her daybed nest of books everyone
jokes about but she can't live without, she tucks herself in to sleep.

> *Whose hearts pounding hers she doesn't know.*
> *Two. Brothers or fathers loved ones she can't tell.*

*Must've flown in the open door like swallows
crashing glass thinking it a barn poor dears
so many lost barns. Spent--it's that time -- they
are spent from coming so far and so far still to go.
Not swallows, rarer. Exquisite in their exhaustion
she's never seen them so close, their wings collapsed
across her heart as books she's fallen asleep reading.
In and out of dream it seems she sometimes
can't tell them apart. She only knows the one
of their hearts so good against hers fearing
if she even whispers they will disappear.*

*She doesn't know how long they are with her only
the weight and quivers of their wings. Handsome,
they let her take them in her hands to witness
but because she can't keep her eyes open, they keep
floating back to her heart. She tries and tries
in her mind's ear to hear what they say dreaming
back and back to their sighs she hears over and over,
again and again. In moments of suspense, she
holds herself in their sense settling which is which,
turning back to each to hear what they seem
to be wanting her to find of themselves before sleep.
What they want her to hear for the rest of her days:*
                                        *her own heart
just as she wants them to hear her "I know, I know.
                                Now go, now go."*

Dreaming something flown, she feels quills spilling again
down the pine. In first snow she longs to go with them a way,
their hearts nearly bursting, the three of them, in a feathery flurry
beyond the four directions the Penobscot long ago showed them
how to find.

Finding where all the light they will ever need can be found,
to see them through this last or any winter of a hundred *a thousand*,
she returns to the sweetest deep sleep in time.

MIXED-HEART MAINE
(Sewing with Old Points)

Sharp, the way bone and horn splinters served, and quills,
until metal people brought theirs in their bodices with other
jewel tools. The way your Scots hurt, too, Bear, blistering
their skin living here. Stitching together necessities for use
and art though never calling it that until museums said *wait*
and saved it.

My worn hands can't punch this needle the hundreds of stitches
it would take to outline your wedding at that dear shore
along Birch Stream the way I still see it, though it's my longest,
finest-pointed one with an eye wide enough to carry the floss
the way our eyes were wide in witness that day taking it in,
still seen. Oh there was a day as you know, how I could've
embroidered the whole rite – you and Susanne in her willow-
natured gown, her hair a long reed-gold breeze. You, a dressed up
bear in a same-shade shirt, rising tall the way our black bears do
to behold this heaven that is earth, opening your Spirit Hill robe
to her. Your hands bound with sweetgrass the way Scots
and Indians still do who reclaim the old clan ways, as if the same
country because the same continent once split in two.

Beloveds, I can't picture all that on this chamois leather
with your family, even Hans and Sarah and Alex, Mama and us,
without my fingers bleeding and back knotting, my arm already
throbbing, though I would for the joy of that day if I didn't know
you two will look at your hands here, traced from those echoes
to this, and ever, and how your fingers are laced the way they were
that day, and ever, and you'll fill it in with own memoried threads
whether I finish this or not but look how much I could do.

Let it be a small shawl for your hard nights and days
for I have lifted it each dawn over these fields you have loved,
to infuse and empower it with my hands, praying for strength.

A sacred skin from love blessed that day and all our days
for I have cradled it in the smoke here in the yard you have loved
that it will carry this place to you to tell you you shall always
be here, this place always with you.

The fur-black and birch-green felt hands you two let me trace
around yours, braided together and appliqued anciently to sign
where you were and why and who else saw and heard, hold
the vision though I can stitch only this much.

Let it be your comfort, your medicine, your health
to cover your heart or rest your head. Look at it and see
all my hands couldn't sew – the water you became together,
the other shore you reached with its standing people applauding,
the eagles we all willed to bring ancestors.

And when it comes time in the flow of time for which there is
no word, when we can no longer see, whether through tears
or other natural veil, touch it the way you did her and
hear John Bear declare you wed again, and again,
even when we all are gone. *All my relations.*

BY THE SOUND

(listening for loons)

Hark to them, the long paired,
when they break the still
which can be peace, or instinct and fear.

Hark to their quiets
and comings together when they do
with signals only they know the meanings to.

How they court the way they first did,
all the more in the sensing one may soon
be gone. Just their wakes everywhere
across the waters of their years together.

Their scars are not all clear.
They know one another's wonders and wounds.
The way they repair.

Some shore night before long one will wail
and be the only one in the shivery surrounds
to hear the reply.

from ANOTHER LONG (70.)

she kisses
the sun rising
for her this morning
their cells dawn
and night sings
it has come
to this

NO END TO IT

Road crew's cut 'n' ground the ash saplings
the birds seeded along the front I'd planned to carve.
That tumbledown roughsawn fence needs replacin'
somethin' awful exposed like that. Just tryin'
to keep somethin' between us and traffic
since they widened the road comin' so close
and bein' the north side needin' to break the wind
no insulation this old part of the ell and right here
can tell where she's comin' from.
Wish for woods between us but our row of hemlock
and pine will have to do, fillin' in, if they'll leave it be.
And the highbush cranberries drawin' the birds I watch
over my desk when it's not too cold in this back room.
But the pulp and gravel pit trucks barrelin'
down Cotton Hill need a clear view I know
and cars bent on hell can't bring themselves to slow
with all the places they've gotta go and the linemen
needin' to keep the lines free lest they come down
in the ice and snow just have to keep an eye.

This damn roof needs doin' again.
We're gettin' too old for this. Don't want him up there
this time. But he's stubborn and will do for himself
won't ask for help by God. Have to call on the kids
to talk some sense into 'im. Lend a hand.

All I ask is to get our stuff cleared out before we die
so the kids won't have to, the someday we might need
it for gone but for what will go into the quilts.
Old board floors just fine and there's comfort
in the old plaster still showin' in the hall and upstairs,
like proof, if we can just get a window we can climb out.
This old place would go up like Baghdad
not that we aren't careful but the old wires, squirrels,

*the old chimneys needin' repair. Our share of chimney
terrors, flames rocketin' into the sky, this old place nothin'
but tinder if not for the boys from the Station out town
workin' both the cellar and roof one more time.
Don't think we don't worry.*

GLIMPSES

After the raccoon gutted one of our last two hens
        out pecking and scratching the spent garden for seeds and bugs

before the freeze, we'd find her partner pressed against the panes
        on the porch day after day. Not that she wanted *in*, nor would

she accept any comfort from voice or hand. After terror, she
        needed her other. To see an image holding her own, so together

they'd become. So one. So this is how it will be,
        living out our times seeking mirrors in glass and pools, unable

to doubt reflections? Unable to see ourselves as alone
        as we will be? Clutching at the slightest movement,

shadow, flicker, fragment, however unbreachable?
        However hard whatever we are up against, however

when we crash to kiss it jars us through the hereafter?

BEDDING VOWS

Confessing in abiding peace, darling,
I'm sorry for any way I let us down today.
Thank you for every effort you've made for us.
My love for you stills and heals my daylight and sleep.
Here's this drop of oil for your heart.
I kiss and hold you, to store what I can of us, joined
and rejoicing, against the grateful grief when,
time to come, it will be our turn for one of us
to carry on alone.

≈ Lot Two ≈

BEING CONSEQUENTIAL & EVERGREEN TESTAMENTS

*What am I thinking? Nothing, actually.
By now I'm completely out of my head.
These are not thoughts at all but the fires
of June speaking even at this time of life.*

– Dana Wilde

*Old mistress Maine she makes you lug lug lug
she makes you pull pull pull she makes you haul
haul haul and when she's thrashed you a plenty between
those thrashings / she's lovely / she smiles / she's beautiful
Maine makes or breaks....*

– John Marin

They loved the nights and dared the days....

– Ruth F. Harrison

*How will you cross
the lonely autumn mountain
alone? It was hard for us,
even when we went together.*

– Princess Oku

HUSBAND CUT MY HAIR

I cannot reach it anymore. Fetch the wedding-dress scissors
from my sewing chest, my good pair to be used only for cloth,
from their blue velvet case. I know it shocks you I would ask,
the way I've guarded it these years letting and letting it lengthen
just for us to dance around my round hips if you still love it lie
with me now and help me let it down as long as...

and weave your fingers through these threads of me husband
if you have loved it slip again into my waves let me be your rings.
Show it as it has shown you. Dip again into its flow is it fabric
or water it doesn't know itself or what it means.
Lift it to your lips and thank it as I have every day.

These tears...*oh*...because of where these fibers of my being
have been what vision settled into them what shine
they may not know again *I cannot reach it anymore.*

If you've loved the way I've carded and plied it by hand
until it's spun a stellar spray down our backs, give your hands
for it to tremble into and look upon it the way a man sighs as if
he will die unless he does. Cup it like our brook being swept away
if it is that and drink it with me as it goes.

Have you loved the way the silver has swirled through the last
of my girl-black silk *whisper that.* The way I've fluted it up
into fountains being my own kind of lady if I have been yours
> *hold me*
> *cut my hair my strength*

> *I cannot reach it anymore.*

SEREIN/RAIN FROM AN APPARENTLY CLOUDLESS SKY
(The Season of Your Growth)

1√
Is tonight's shocking moon because you, husband, have seen
the rusting cordwood saw rising as an electric star in your guts?
Or is it the fire I've built you from every power (within reach
and summonsed) risen? The smoke a whispered supplication?

2√
Our first morning knowing cracks open with a thunder and lightning
downpour we are smack in the middle of. *Oh boys of our early love, come
and return the sun.* Pounding all day. The hen house gets shingled. Trim
painted. You ask for cake half joking. This is new for you something
this wrong inside your own timbered frame. I do the pineapple upside
down one in the cast iron spider I haven't made since the children
were small and the heat shattered the milk glass pedestal I'd saved S & H
green stamps for so long. They bring ice cream everything dream.
The calendar turns heavy as the milk house you once moved
a side at a time on your back.

3√
All day you build with the boys you can't stop.
Next, a float for camp . . . yes . . . *we'll float through this* . . . .
At day's end, instead of turning in, you decide we'll go for supplies
for the ladder you'll make to it tomorrow it's not too late I'll go any-
where with you anytime. Otherworldly mists in the valleys the whole
way make us wish for our camera – *we must remember.* Last night's
full night-sun moon has returned weaker, shouldering us safely home
fiddling as ever for right words. Tonight we'll try sleeping by the pond.

4√
See how the fire I have risen in the night to build us against the camp's
damp turns the stove into a jack-o-lantern flickering in the dark as if
yesterday's horseshoe clanks and cheers and laughter over the water
and dueling hallelujah fireworks across the pond we drifted off on

were a trick. The surprising insect (I suspect) (or fairy) lights over the bog
flying there and there and there must wonder about the fireflies
(from cracks in the stove's seams) in here. When you wake I shall barely
skim the skillet with pure butter and brown you the oatmeal-molasses
dough risen all night and patty-caked to go with yesterday's clover-fed
eggs and green tea in defense. The turtles, of course, know nothing
of this. Nor the ghostly loon looming in dawn fog just off shore.

5√
One day crows into another into one long lung that keeps catching.
You spread litter in the coop and secure the roost. Nail double screens
over the windows against predators driven to gnash and rip and suck
and bring them in with their water and grain. I scythe clover
they tread not knowing what else to do needing a mother.
I should call yours I keep thinking, years gone the way of rain within.

6√
You say they haven't used their roost poor things.
You're right, let's put a hen with them these chicks sent away for
knowing only themselves boxed in. Not like the banties hatching
already knowing pecking orders and how to scratch and fend.
How many generations, these, bred away from even the cellular
memory of grass not to mention sun? Not even getting what
their little flap door is for let alone the green run you shape for them
outside through the hay. Sweat trickles from your face and neck
what remarkable fortune having had such a father
wishing we could call yours gone too.

7√
Ellsworth for car repairs. Meandering, dazed, waiting for something
to open. No benches for resting. We dodge High Street traffic for seats
in front of the laundry and Reny's, buying a paring knife for fifty cents.
Then back over the lanes to Bean's to spend our coupons, no place
to cross without risk. People on feet beware. Gas-fueled vehicles
required and sometimes it seems we'll enlist our country's children
to kill and be killed to keep it this way more every day.
But just-picked strawberries for sale on the Chicken Barn road home
and three old pals from out of the blue call with their life news
including a French daughter one didn't know he had and do you golf?

Lunching with them over the harbor in Castine do you wonder about
your life about which they know nothing? Back home will your supper
of hot-from-the-oven buttered biscuit shortcakes with these sweet fruits
be enough?

8√
You want to write of it in me day after day and I pray to read
every word you spill. No free sleep anymore only the need
for safe roosts. And dreams. Morning and night we face the Mystery,
grateful for whatever is shown.

> *This is how it comes to me: So sacred a visitation*
> *I can write only this much for now in trust.*
> *I've arrived at a house upriver full with women.*
> *All ages of what my DNA figures I am – all four races*
> *the way we looked before separation. My Penobscot*
> *medicine friend is at home being shown where she belongs*
> *by elders but I am like the chickens in their new place*
> *uncovering late all they are, what I was born hearing*
> *though not why, what it meant, keeping my place.*
> *From all the way around the flows we've called Time*
> *these women have come dressed in history's clothes,*
> *their ways comforting old. The ageless African*
> *with most reverence about her bids us (in foreign*
> *tongue I somehow grasp the meaning of) say*
> *who we are what we need. Her rows of hair gather*
> *straight back. Her face is quartered with root, sinew,*
> *fibers, incision, stain or tattoo. I fear to call her mine*
> *but she dreams to me she is. (Husband here beside me*
> *can you hear?) The young Inuit one nursing her infant*
> *finishes her story with ". . . and my mother just died."*
> *My hand flies to my mouth not stopping my cry*
> *to which she smiles sad recognition we are sisters.*
> *(You, husband, finally asleep, did you dream them too*
> *showing me what I need to know to help us fiercely*
> *and serenely to the other side of this threat?*
> *Can you see the seams in my face located tonight?*
> *Original woman before the loss of natural knowledge?*
> *All womanly wisdoms joined?*
> *Beloved, you must draw deep from your soul your way.)*

*My Indian Island sage says this means the grand-
mothers are with us, bringing this message for healing
I cannot yet wholly tell.*

9√
Hearts arrive in the mail. The telephone returns to a music box.
Friends gather without us, our names safe on their tongues.
You disappear down the corridor....wait....*wait*....our children
and I wait while the scanner scans. Then home to wait.
You ask me to play the piano for you. Shadows spread, falling
on the news.

10√
Sisters and brothers fly in from the west bringing feathers
and books. We gather in a homestead whose spirits remember us
and build prayer fires in and out not that we ask for preferential
treatment but only for right hearts to find natural medicines near
and the best science we can afford in these parts.

11√
Some days . . . who knows what happens . . . .

12√
After mowing, raking, shoveling, spreading,
(anything thinkable to help or not) – woodpile, vegetables,
well house, camp – the elders gather at the shore, pace,
play word games after dark, and shudder.

13√
Days and nights meld. Sisters rock in the boat
facing the sun speaking grandmothering and new birth.
Your grandfather spirit lifts over the pond.
We drink all afternoon, intoxicating ourselves with well water
laughing and hurting, everything ritual.

14√
Images await, not caring what we want.
The children cook for four generations. Feathers over the table.
Stones in the center. The youngest drums.

15√
All night – rain, roof.
You have not slept I rise before light.
It is the earliest it has ever been. The clock points and we go.

16√
Dawn is dark and not entirely benign.

17√
Malignancy in high places.

18√
After everything, camp. The two of us laughing
in the hammock. Pitch in my hair. Brother's pipes
off the dock. Sisters' round bottoms over the boat's side.
Reflections doubling everything. Our old mother listening.
A warming.

19√
Some can't stay, we know. But the ruby-glittered slipper
from Kansas we carry back and forth, taking turns with, remains.
And when we return from meeting with neighboring campers
and the state on the higher than ever water and beaver-deceiving
strategies for our forested wetland, we find a new flashlight and
swimming noodles we'll ride if we can bring ourselves to.
Their absence floods.

20√
How many trips through the woods to the airport upriver
to bring them home, take them back, to fly away again year after year?

This time, kids back from Iraq. Why are we here I cry I can't recall.
One's waiting to call his dad who lost his legs in Vietnam. Mississippi
boy face brown as the doll we got our kids. I could be his grandmother
I see through raining eyes.

Hello, coming or going? Ah, brief leave. So thankful you made it home.
How each war since the world one I was born to we thought

we'd finally learned how to do things better without war.
Yes, he lowers his eyes and replies, we sure learned a lot about that,
how we should've done things, it'll never be over . . . .

I hope your life is good from now on, son.

Thank you take this.... his frayed armband I.D. he signs
as if pleading *remember me please don't forget me.*

I won't, Tyree, I promise I won't!

21√
Given but one more day of life, what would we do?
Water rising, rising.

22√
Our boys gather their prying tools, cant dog, peavey,
crow bars, mason's hoe and father
and meet the game warden for their permit, steering the boat
behind the island out of sight. Now the pond will flow free,
sink below the dock again, recede from the steps and under
the camp back into the bog. The brook runs once more.
But the beavers, relentless and masterful like you, will return
after dark and rework it. The more it rains, their signal, the more
they build, being beavers, but there is balance here again. Balance.
All any of us desire.

23√
The lone loon surfaces beside our canoe showing us
how not to be afraid, stand up to fear, run fiercely on what
can drown, its white-spotted black feathers shedding water
in its dinosaurian red-eyed haunt.

24√
Work. Work. Prepare, but for what? The young ones gather
us near in thick loss for what else to do.

25√
Your longest brother and sister bringing treats, hopes, memories,

Lumberjack tees, knitting, strengths of spirits gone on. More work.

26√
Oh daughter of our earliest love, may your wings bring you and your boy, which is to say ours, safely from the Pacific rim to our arms.

27√
We paddle to the west cove to check the level.
Pond smooth as oil. Behind the island through the reeds
we see the underwater grasses straining forward with the current,
the breach holding. Swamp roses. History. What it must've been like
before our kind. Surf up all the way back to our low lot.
Soup. *And peace attend thee all through the night....*

28√
Oh don't go yet to the light!

29√
For the surgeon to weed your tubers
may his hands be as true as yours.

30√
Remember how we gussied up for our first fancy dance
like those kids playing dress-up on that get well card?
You in your hard-earned man suit and onyx high school
commencement ring with sparkling speck gentlemaning
your handsome baseball hands, grand to me in wonder-
land white lady-gloves up to my elbows over strapless
black taffeta ballet gown with whispering petticoats
buying on time knowing against all proof we were
for a fact rich? And how through the years, looking back,
we started saying we were just little buggers? *Oh grand-
children, like you!*

31√
Instructions / assurances / day for fire at dawn /dried mountain
laurel twigs saved from your ancestral home / pressed cedar and
pine boughs with your mother's last breaths / paper balls of fire
in my hands strongest ever felt /even rain-wet logs making it

to ash /wend of smoke up through your open window / no dif--
ference between hair and smoke detected in embraces at hospital /
family prayer encircling / holding / you.

32√
Button found at Grasshopper Shop for your johnny which
is to say journey: *What if the hokey pokey IS what it's all about?*

33√
Anesthesia / sliced flesh / your kidney / your adrenal /
your lymph nodes / your radical nephrectomy / the chapel /
the clock / the surgeon's mouth.

34√
Reunion!

35√
You walk again, all pain / the thanksgivings /the strengths
of the children / how love looks / how the sky.

36√
Blue moon / everything double batched.

37√
Dawns after, the whole horizon is a bruised incision
not stapled like you but sewn by our family bats tatting
in first light back and forth over and over until it is done
and I go out to your potato patch to collect the beetle larvae
devouring the leaves that *make no mistake* will kill.
The changed children come to help.

Have we found them all? HAVE WE?

UP THROUGH THIS FALLING DARK
A 70-STAR CONSTELLATION

Some spy the night sky
hunting dippers and bears,

but the moons he's roofed into,
the seventh decade of his earthly years,

have taken him in as he has them,
pounding without ceasing, keeping

a roof over his family's heads.
Securing his staging higher

and ever higher, he has earned
the constellation they see as his.

Roll after tarred roll, shingle
by glinting shingle, he has nailed down

his spirit which is to say nailed up,
giving all he has had to give

before turning to death. Worrying,
his wobbly wife takes up her kind

of night-hued felt, snips a black
silhouette top to their old ark

with its yee-yaw chimneys and eaves,
and hand stitches it across her

twilight's blue, neat as he's worked his
rows his whole life. Then sews

70 glittering specks, silver-cored glass
aurora borealis seed-beads, into a risen

Ladder and Hammer overhead
amidst a scattered starry surround

to show him how wondrous
he is to them, and what they, hereafter,

will see sparkling in the universe
he has repaired and repaired and repaired.

For his 80th, she will embroider and stud
his garden and woodpile to high heaven,

commencing, with him, in the morning.

POETRY AS WEDDING DRESS: WEDDING DRESS AS POETRY

THE WOMEN FABRICATE THEIR DREAMS

*The honor of your presence is requested by
Designer & Installation Artist, Meredith Alex
&
Mixed-blood Yankee Poet, Patricia Smith Ranzoni
to witness the embodiment of their collaboration
for the Art~Poetry Walk of the 2008 Belfast Poetry Festival*

High Street Gallery   Belfast, Maine

Dearly Beloved, if I may be so bold (as my father would say) ~
Midst confusion and disillusion (what we've clung to in belief slipping
away and away) until no footing remains, we stagger near to witness
a diverse use of Imagination beyond War, Fraud, Greed. We gather
to swear to a desperate form of refusal, and how we can re-pair, if not
save ourselves, if we will but look into each other's work, admitting
what we see. As here, along this high coast procession, wedding
ourselves and others as we wish to be wed. As in this account I tease
your tired ears to hear ~

According to the custom for this annual chance, the elder and younger
are assigned. Committing, they meet by the waterfall just west of the bay.
The young one is late from her Yorkie's morning run-in with a skunk
the color the elder's hair used to be, young and old together, like them.
The elder is late from her sandal-thong letting go. She can't walk without
tripping on her sole. But her old man helps her find her size at the
Goodwill store, striped colors she'd never otherwise choose, freeing her
to meet this new sort of woman without limping and dragging a flopping
shoe. *Oh, God, may she please not be a queen....* Because how does

one born outside the money economy meet a fashion star and installation artist (the elder fears, guessing what that is)?

For gifts, she brings the protective cloaks her books of poems have become. And the priceless fabric they'll come to call Trust.

Sizing one another up--the elder, stout; young, petite--they study for patterns. Tints. Textures. Grains they can believe in. Threads by which their lives have hung. The back of the designer's jeep is stacked with mannequins, dashboard collaged. Like the elder's kitchen wall! And hadn't the elder been making everyday clothes since the grainbag cloth of her youth? And brave and celebratory raiment for family and friends through the years?

Before too long, swapping what they might together explore, the younger locates the elder's cloistral wish for a wedding gown of her own, not for a coronation like so many, not borrowed (because every cent for school), needing to be returned, her sister's city street-length one. Not hers. Not her.

But an original interpretation of a life's love and love's life. Poetry for wearing! In the sheer yardage unfolding and gathering between the eyes of the elder and younger, their dared visions seam into a swirl all whispers, hums, laughter and cheers worthy of this dancey canvassed High Street company, even (*listen*) the North Atlantic Blues.

Fitting the designer's calendar, they meet next at the elder's table across the river to the east, confessing they recognize one another--women whose time has come if they but choose--seeing they need only spin and cherish to their chests their own hopes, as long as they both shall live.

Easy as pie for the younger to want to make the dress the elder never had. If, after, she'd teach her how to make this blueberry kind. Tablecloths! the younger sings, scanning the farm. Bring me table lace! So, saving for gas, she will soon return to Belfast, the elder and her other, with totes of faith from her lifelong stash, including well-worn passed along damask that might become a train, wishing just the same for

scraps of the outing flannel her mother made diapers with upriver at 7
cents a yard to tuck someplace maybe as wildflowers. Before plumbing,
electricity, vehicle, calling forth their one kerosene lamp, enough for the
tar-papered cabin her father'd built for them back there. A rich,
crash-proof life on which she still banks. For same reasons,
she envisions a secret garter of cobalt and black checked flannel
representing their sapphire anniversary she bought it for but didn't
get made, for her Maine woman's heart. Maybe embellished
with the inky-blue glass one from her sister on the plains.

For enspiriting her gown she brings grandmother pictures the younger
will iron down two flaring gores in front. And crochetwork, pillowcase
tatting, runners and doilies standing for her mother's mother Hattie
of Castine and their *Mayflower* strain, who, after Meadow Farm sold,
years to come, kept house and cooked for a jeweler right here
in Belfast; Hattie's mother Ethel of Orland who raised Captain Snow-
man's nine, his ship since 18 off to the Caribbean; Edith Demuth
of the Old Broad Bay German colony becoming Waldoboro, mother
of the elder's grandfather Young who composed and conducted the
Rockland City and Damariscotta bands. Then, great great grandmother,
Sophronia, who fabricated her family's very survival (after her caulker
mate plunged to death from rigging at the Brewer ship yard) making
mens' britches by hand for 50 cents a pair down to Leaches Point where
she had to move.

Father's side – orphaned Helen Viola, daughter of Angus MacLellan
come from Canada. A Parker Ridge New Brunswick domestic, daughter
of Christina Snow of Mic Mac eyes carried away in her thirties in
influenza's gauze, Angus off to Minnesota. And great grandmother
Myrie who wove baskets and rocked on the stairs to the sick children's
chambers singing lullabies, and her moccasin and tradecloth-wearing
mother Abenlena, tied to the tribes out Pickle Ridge, Webster Planta-
tion, where she lived with the Indians. Middle ground where Passama-
quoddy and Penobscots pieced themselves back together. Sacred wear
she prizes with them. And a cherished saucer-size hairlace made
the traditional way by Breton fingers brought from France by a friend.
Maybe for basting over her heart.

And these storied beads in blues collected one by one following family coast to coast. Like these hundred year old egg-size agate cattle-keeper beads from *Africa Adorned* that make the elders laugh remembering the hard time they decided not to part because *what about the cows?* And this hummingbird nest-size seed-beaded sling carrying a beach gem from their girl's Pacific rim. This remnant of sleek sealskin from her Quoddy Bay history and rabbit fur from her husband's ancestral ground along the Mohawk Trail. Partridge feathers illustrating her "Pine Hen" poem whose words will flow down her curtain veil they'll each print a hand on, elder and younger, symbolizing joined power; and feathers found by her husband, brother and sisters, sons and grandchildren, wherever they go: wild turkey, loon, jay, teal-winged duck from the moose hunt up north. A fragrant pine spray for her hair.

All she prays is not to look like an aspiring queen her ancestors rose against, dissidents by DNA. Or like an old woman trying to look young, being eternally grateful for having endured. No longer to die early the way she once felt she would. Vintage, that's what she is, vintage, thankful for the folds in her knotted tapestry skin and age-marks worn by her expressions, healed thorn gouges from blackberrying, well-worn hands, and the emptying well of ink she's written from her once-sooty hair.

River crossing by river crossing, exchange by exchange, the women fabricate their dreams. The elder, astonished what the younger can show, how she can know, answers, "Wand Woman, hearing your reverence for my 'Bedding Vows,' yes, my answer is yes," pledging 'if when it comes time you still want me to marry you in the historic practice of poet as Justice of the Peace, with rites you help write, when the lucky still-unknown-to-you man who will fix your vegetable bin and look at you as more than another lobster feast will know that entering your being will be like entering your high lemon-chiffon home with its three flights lined with recycled earth-saving shoes and accessories up through a festival of teens (the elder brings molasses corn balls for) and artful articles, all the way to the top floor where fantastical inventions and accents fly off needing no doors. Garments from materials never thought possible. "She is a poet, making everything new," the elder sees. Where the whole place is her conjuring space so her press can stay hot as needed and this row of ruffles here and this soft mound of silk here

and these poms and sequins here and this explosion of energy here.....
Bodices, dress forms, busts everywhere. Notions, chain, netting, cork,
fluff. To live with her is to live with transformative stuff deeply
in the acrobatic art of it. And, reciprocally, the creations of friends.

Fabricating their dreams, the younger offers how *her* wedding gown
"will rip off in a mad kiss to reveal the polka dot party dress signifying
the official party-in-partnership has begun ....*kiss kiss busy busy....*" And
may it last through two rings like the elder's old man's. Gold, then silver,
worn through against wood, machines, stones, metal, tools, on hands
that, like hers, never cease. Last long enough for looking back over like
they, the elder and her mate. Reasons she'll weave her sweetgrass braid
with vine from his arbor, binding a wrist-fitting "hand fasting" wreath
in the ancient way of her clan in Scotland and her Penobscot relations
marrying to this day at Birch Stream. How the new volume, *Baskets of
the Dawnland People*, teaches that the same species of sweetgrass
that grows here grows over there, called "holy grass" for scattering
along paths to church, fastened over marrying hands in the ritual
believed to birth the saying, "tying the knot."

Around hers she purls long flowing white twill ribbon fringe for attaching the symbols of who they've been as people that they didn't know
when they pledged *they did* and *would* nearing fifty years ago. The
marriage of all the racial origins of the world, loving more than themselves. An Italian pewter stag button from his grandparents' alpine land
and denoting how he still provides. Their sterling French Huguenot
cross with pendant dove for the Holy Ghost commemorating their
survival of persecutions, both sides, his and hers. Her Wabanaki ash
and sweetgrass needle case from her mother's dowry. The first Native-made silver brooch her poetry earned to strengthen her voice.
A postage-stamp size book locket he bought after her first collection
where she keeps a note of recognition from a Bear. The wire heart he
gave her with three bells for their children and the music necessary
to their lives. A primary-colored Mali wedding bead for each decade,
found on the other side. Her MacLellan clan pin will fasten her tartan
over her arm. The something Asian will adorn her feet, the young one's
cutwork napkin lace arabesqueing her shoes' toes from whatever bridge

across land, water, sky; and these five fat turquoise rounds for the family made with their children.

See frantic last minute trimming....pinning....stitching....and might they dare imagine a photograph for ancestors after? A portrait if money can be found?

Finally, (sliding the "fasting" wreath over their clasped hands), the two pronounce her ribbon-tied prayers, the dressmaker and street procession their witnesses-of-honor in the gallery that wind-chilled passersby notice glows as a ceremonial grotto with community fire to warm them through another winter's long. Thusly:
(*after James Wright's "Complaint"*)
Elder wife:
Knowing this day will come, we've cried and laughed and together put these down.

> *He's done. He was my heart, my wine, and more.*
> *He kept the squirrels out and braced the floor,*
> *scraped up the cores and peelings after pies,*
> *and shamed the children never to tell lies.*
> *Now strapping boys have grown past mischievous.*
> *And our girl's son pays back her devilishness.*
> *So they can see we made our strongest home*
> *and see us in themselves in time to come.*
> *Still, while sweet nephews with their city wives*
> *dream to hunt and lead their country lives,*
> *what back will shore the house, what hands will jam*
> *and stack dry oak for fires to keep it warm?*
> *And who will clean the henhouse, dress the rows,*
> *and skin and cut the buck for this year's stews?*
> *Not my old man who gladly did such toil,*
> *to sweat and guard our lives from out this soil*
> *and stack cord wood for fires past earthly sore.*
> *For now he rests, who was my sun but more.*

Elder husband:
> *She's through. She was my rock, my chick, and more,*
> *She tracked the mice and moths and mopped the floor.*
> *She made the pies and all the breadly goods.*
> *She wanted words and put nuts in my food.*
> *She taught the children love with elders first*
> *and oft times asked for only songs and verse.*
> *And when they'd grown and had kids of their own,*
> *she paced and cried and wrung her hands again.*
> *And when far nieces turned away from soil,*
> *she told them where they came from and the toil.*
> *Now what voice will call us to come and sit*
> *and what white hair will rise to meet the light?*
> *And who will clean the cupboards, mend my pants,*
> *and dig the greens and calm my foolish rants?*
> *Not my old babe who asked for just a kiss*
> *to touch and keep our lives for times like this*
> *and stoke the fires of home past earthly sore.*
> *For now she rests, who was my chick and more.*

Somewhere over the river, between some moon and some dawn, this dress's and poem's Will will be done

as, now, here,
we have begun.

ANSWERING WHAT MIGHT BE ECHOES OF AN OLD MALISEET SONG NOT MINE

Look oft up the river, look oft and oft.

I watch over the water, I watch over and over.

In spring at ice-out, I watch over.

Do you see me coming across in your canoe?

I watch over the water, I watch for you, for you.

ACKNOWLEDGMENTS

Citations below constitute an extension of the copyright page.

All of these poems and segments from sectional poems, worked and published from the early 1980s to the present, have appeared or are forthcoming in the following paper and electronic journals and collections whose editors have my gratitude.

Aputamkon Review * *a handful of stones* (U.K.) * *A Sense of Place, Collected Maine Poems* (Bay River Press, 2002) * *Bigger Stones* * *Bucksport Enterprise* * *Christian Science Monitor* * *CLAIMING, Poems by Patricia Ranzoni* (Puckerbrush Press, 1995) * *Curio Poetry* * *Earthshine* * *Echoes, The Northern Maine Journal* * *FarmHouse Magazine* * *Felt Sun* * *Fried Chicken and Coffee* * *Gravity* * *Half Way Down The Stairs* * *HIBERNACULUM & Other North-natured Poems by Patricia Ranzoni* (OneWater Press, 2010) * *Illness & Grace, Terror & Transformation* (Wising Up Press, 2007) * *Kaleidoscope: International Magazine of Literature, Fine Arts, and Disability* * *Monongahela Review* * *Narramissic Notebook* * *Off the Coast* * *ONLY HUMAN ~ Poems from the Atlantic Flyway by Patricia Ranzoni* (Sheltering Pines Press, 2005) * *Out of the Cradle* * *Passion and Pride: Poets in Support of Equality* (Moon Pie Press, 2012) * *Patricia Ranzoni: Greatest Hits 1982-2008* (Greatest Hits Series #273, Pudding House Publications, 2009) * *Poetry Addicts* * *Poetry Scotland* (U.K.) * *Poetry Tonight* * *Poet's Market 1998* * *Prayers to Protest, Poems That Center and Bless Us* (Pudding House Publications, 1998) * *Puckerbrush Review* * *Red Booth Review* * *Saltwater Quarterly* * *Scythe* * *SETTLING, Poems by Patricia Ranzoni* (Puckerbrush Press, 2000) * *Son of Fat Tuesday* * *Sweet Annie & Sweet Pea Review* * *The Green Hills Literary Lantern* * *Tuesday, Oregon Coast Anthology* * *Uni-Verse/Bangor Daily News* * *Untitled Country Journal* * *Viaggio di Gioia/Journey of Joy, poems to carry & give to Monteviasco by Patricia Ranzoni* (OneWater Press, 2010) * *Vine-Leaves Journal* (AUS) * *Wild Violet Magazine* * *Wolf Moon* * *Words & Images* * *Yankee Magazine*

Thanks to Jeff Gamelin and Paulann Petersen whose images I've gratefully invited to converse with mine under poem titles, with their permissions. Further, please note these credits for words borrowed for the "Lot" dividers:

Dana Wilde for lines from "Within a Budding Grove," from his "Amateur Naturalist" column (*Bangor Daily News*, 2010), and *The Other End of the Driveway, An amateur naturalist's observations in the Maine woods* (Booklocker. com, Inc., 2012).

Ruth F. Harrison for her line from "Brief Story" from *Year With No Summer* (Cape Perpetua Press, 2008).

Dorothea Honora Moulton Balano's 1912 lines from *The Log of the Skipper's Wife* by James W. Balano (Down East Books, 1979) used by permission of John Balano, literary executor, and Down East Books.

Lines from "First Song" from *Pairs* by Philip Booth, copyright © 1994 by Philip Booth, are used by permission of Penguin, a division of Penguin Group (USA) Inc.

Lines as noted are from John Marin's 1932 letter to Stieglitz No. 144, *The Selected Writings of John Marin*, Edited with an Introduction by Dorothy Norman (Pellegrini & Cudahy, 1949), from *Internet Archive*.

Princess Oku (661 – 702), was the daughter of Emporor Temmu of Japan. This ancient expression of love, "How will you cross . . ." is, of course, an interpretation.

For the full text of "Making Maybaskets," written and read for the invitational Centennial of the Ellsworth Maine Public Library Festival of Poets, April 1997; and naming 23 esteemed late and contemporary authors working in Hancock County during the author's childhood and present, see *SETTLING, Poems by Patricia Ranzoni* (Puckerbrush Press, 2000). Thanks again to Millvale neighbor, Julia White Bowden for teaching us the song referred to at the opening of the poem as children on the school bus, and singing it with me at readings. Due to the internet, we now know it should be attributed to songwriter, Cy Coben. Lines 6 – 11 in stanza two appreciate William Carpenter's "The Ecuadorian Sailors" from *Rain* (Northeastern University Press, 1985). Documentation of "Bucksport's rare wild rose yarrow," same section, comes from the rare little volume, *Seaside Yarrow ~ A Bucksport Story*, by Robert L. Parker, discovered at Buck Memorial Library through Geraldine Spooner. Charlotte Elliot (1789 - 1871) authored the text, and William B. Bradbury the tune to "The Gospel" ("Just as I am. . .") from which I've quoted eight words. Reference to "Howl" is a nod to Allen Ginsberg and the "beat" poets from their far world. Lines from "Barnacle Bill the Sailor" derive from variations of that bawdy old shanty. Fragments from Henry Wadsworth Longfellow's "The Village Blacksmith" and "Evangeline, A Tale of Acadie," and Alfred Noyes's "The Highwayman" echo generations of elementary school and life-long memorizations reflecting the esteemed place of poetry here, a pleasure we take to this day as naturally as we revel in other essential food.

My closing husband-wife stanzas of "Poetry as Wedding Dress : Wedding Dress as Poetry" play most respectfully with the spirit and form of James Wright's distinguished poem, "Complaint" from *James Wright: Selected Poems* (Farrar, Straus, and Giroux and Wesleyan Press).

"Answering What Might Be Echoes / of An Old Maliseet Song Not Mine" is my heart's response to "Maliseet Love-Song," heard all the way across the continent from home, in an antiques shop in my daughter's village in Oregon, while completing this collection; reportedly recorded by ethnomusicologist, Natalie Curtis, as published in *The Indians' Book: An offering by the American Indians of Indian lore, musical and narrative, to form a record of the songs and legends of their race* (Harper and Brothers, 1907).

Wholehearted thank yous to Patricia Newell and North Country Press for doing unto my work this way. And to Joey Ranzoni and Johnny Graveline, Gina and Wayne Tapp, Hazel and Hutch Hutchinson, and Ernie Smith for patient technological help making it possible. This book would have been all the harder without the moral support of my sons and their families; of my mother, on the way to 97, in the midst of memorizing "The Cremation of Sam Magee" (Robert William Service); and of my sisters, Linda and Paula. Not least by any means, I'll always acknowledge with life-altered gratitude, Steve Jobs and Co., in this season of his death, for making it possible, from 1984, for hands to write which could not without Apples, including mine.

Above all, I am beholden to the source of these poems: a half-century-plus partnership with Ed Ranzoni, "Papa Ranza" (and family born from life with him), through which we've learned together, by way of discoveries and trials, marriage and re-marriage, how some love is and does. A relationship, maybe, like Robert Frost is said to have believed a good poem should be – beginning in delight and ending in wisdom. And, I might add, fortunate the fun and pain between. *Oh sing a song of differences! This, but also this!*

Thank you, generous considerers of my work, like the distinguished photographer-scholar, Arthur Ollman, who pictured our rooting partnership as a young neighbor on his "back to the land" sojourn through Maine on the way to his own beloved. Those who, like Ollman, see and respect how word pictures of partners, like poetic photographs to which he has devoted life, are "about personal exposure. This is where the camera shoots in both directions." (Ollman, Arthur, *The Model Wife*, Bulfinch Press. 1999). Gladly quoted with his outback-loving consent. For same reasons, special appreciations to Judy Hakola, John Bear Mitchell, Sanford Phippen, George N. and H.H. Price, and Kimberly Pye for their thoughtful readings and inside cover words.

Abiding thankfulness for the University of Maine at Orono for the relations it confers, and to our State, herself, where students who meet in a zoology class on the Penobscot can find themselves half a century later on the Kennebec sitting next to the professor's son (Dr. Barden's Albie) around the fire among the roots of "The Pines" memorializing the Norridgewock Massacre of 1724.

Thank you, ever – family, friends, strangers – who've through the years honored this place and us, praying to have reflected the same One Love in which we all live here on Earth and after. *PSR*

ஐ The Author ಜಿ

Patricia Smith Ranzoni was born into 1940 up the Penobscot River, before the grid, in Lincoln, Enfield, and Cold Stream country, from the marriage of a young Canadian-American woodsworker from Webster Plantation and a Castine farm girl, both descended from mixed native and European wilderness and border peoples - music and verse revering peoples - as far back as can be found, so far, in what became Maritime Canada and Maine. She grew up with four siblings downriver in Bucksport and Hancock County where her WW II sailor father found work as a rigger at the paper mill. Though she worked her way through bachelor's, master's and certificate of advanced studies degrees in education and counseling at the University of Maine, in which she practiced professionally in public and private settings while homesteading with her husband and three children - saving one of the subsistence farms of her youth - she is unschooled in poetry to which she turned in 1983 when the onset of the neuromuscular disorder, dystonia, began threatening her speech and motor control. Documenting the cultures of her people, her work, published across the United States and abroad, is drawn from for courses and archives of Maine's writers and history, as well as class and disability studies. In 2002 she was the first poet from the northern chain to be invited to read her work at the annual "Women of Appalachia" conference at Ohio University Zanesville. In 2004 University of Maine classmates gave a step in her honor, cited in bronze, toward the renovation of the Fogler Library entrance for whose dedication she composed and read her "Steps". In 2011 she was one of four representing the Maine Folklife Center's "Maine's Farmer Poets" reading at the American Folk Festival in Bangor; and in 2012 she was invited to read at the gala commemorating the 100th anniversary of the discovery of Edna St. Vincent Millay at Whitehall Inn in Camden, was named the first Poet Laureate of the University of Maine Class of 1962, had poems chosen by Maine's Poet Laureate Wesley McNair for his "Take Heart" newspaper columns, and was invited as one of the featured readers in his "Poetry Express" (through Maine) series. In 2014 the Bucksport Town Council named her the town's first poet laureate "for as long as she shall live."

BEDDING VOWS, Love Poems from Outback Maine is Patricia Ranzoni's twelfth title following *WHEREing* (Red Ochre Press, 2011); *VIAGGIO DI GIOIA/Journey of Joy* (author sewn, OneWater Press, 2010); *FROM HERE* (author sewn, OneWater Press, 2010); *HIBERNACULUM & Other North-natured Poems* (author sewn, OneWater Press, 2010); *Patricia Ranzoni ~ GREATEST HITS #273* (Pudding House Press, 2009); *ONLY HUMAN ~ Poems from the Atlantic Flyway* (Sheltering Pines Press, 2005); *LEAVINGS* (Bayriver Press, 2005); *TAKE ME BACK TO SEBEC* (author sewn, 2003); *TRIO: Meaning Three Poems or Maybe One* (broadside, *Buffalo Vortex, 2001*); *SETTLING* (Puckerbrush Press, 2000); and *CLAIMING* (Puckerbrush Press, 1995).

Do you love me or do you not?
You told me once but I forgot.

-Author unknown
Pith & Vinegar

www.ingramcontent.com/pod-product-compliance
Lightning Source LLC
LaVergne TN
LVHW041341080426
835512LV00006B/562